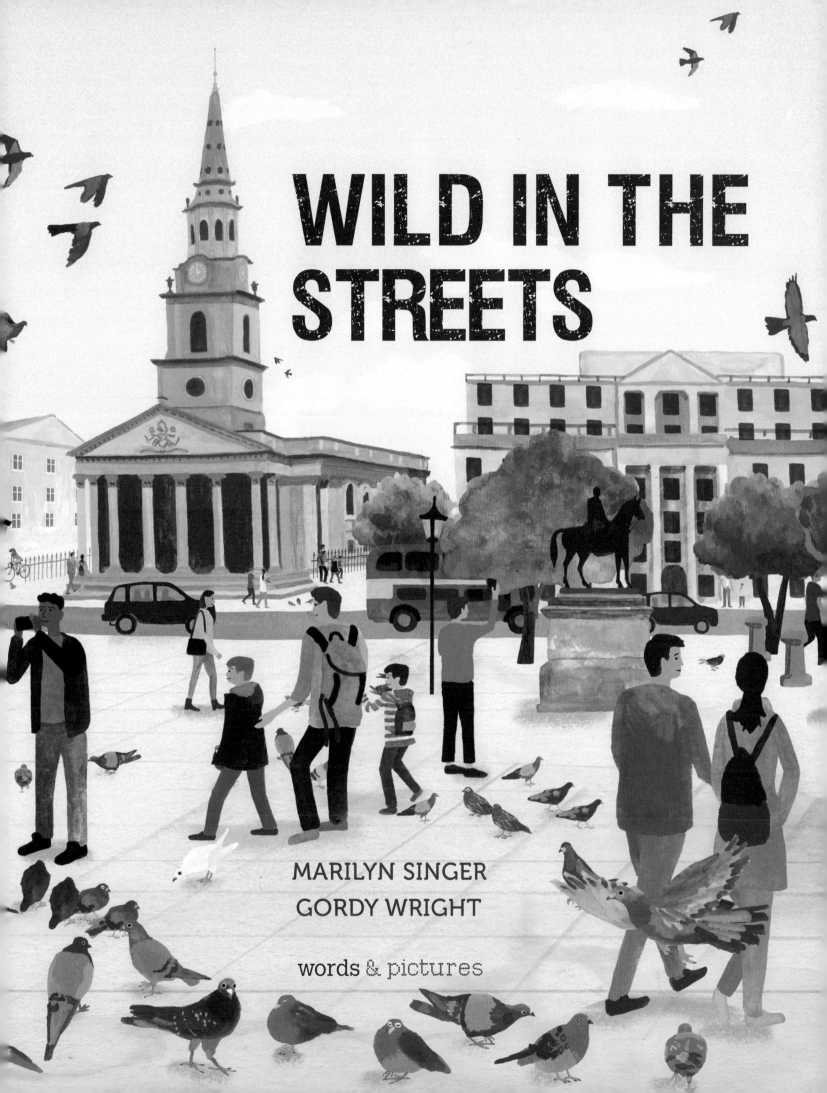

WILD IN THE STREETS

MARILYN SINGER

GORDY WRIGHT

words & pictures

Quarto is the authority on a wide range of topics.
Quarto educates, entertains and enriches the lives of
our readers—enthusiasts and lovers of hands-on living.
www.quartoknows.com

First published in 2019 by words & pictures,
an imprint of The Quarto Group.
6 Orchard Road, Suite 100, Lake Forest, CA 92630.
T: +1 949 380 7510
F: +1 949 380 7575
www.quartoknows.com

Editor: Ellie Brough
Consultant: Michael Bright
Editorial Director: Laura Knowles
Art Director: Susi Martin
Creative Director: Malena Stojic
Publisher: Maxime Boucknooghe

A CIP record for this book is available from the Library
of Congress.

ISBN 978 0 7112 4170 1

Manufactured in Shenzhen, China PP072019

9 8 7 6 5 4 3 2 1

MIX
Paper from
responsible sources
FSC
www.fsc.org
FSC® C001701

PIER 17

Contents

Concrete, glass, tarmac, steel—
who'd imagine they'd appeal
to creatures that once lived
      in forests, caves, on prairies, rocks?
How did they land on city blocks,
under bridges, on rooftops
in playgrounds and drains
      (even in our houses, perhaps when it rains)?
What do they eat? Where do they sleep?
Who are these beings, beloved or reviled?
What wildlife can possibly flourish
      where life's no longer wild?

Introduction

Bats, boars, coyotes, rhesus monkeys, reticulated pythons, huntsman spiders, honeybees, and river crabs. What do all of these animals have in common? They have **adapted** well to city life.

It may be hard to believe that wildlife can survive among densely packed houses, huge skyscrapers, tarmac, sidewalks, and sewers. Yet many species find that urban environments provide ample food, warmth, shelter, and places to raise young, and that these habitats are often similar to their original homes. For example, rock pigeons first came from China, where they lived on cliffs and ledges. City buildings are a fine replacement. Though they are seed-eaters in the wild, pigeons have learned to eat a variety of food found in parks and on roads and streets.

Some urban animals were here before humans encroached on their territory. They've had to adapt to the new habitat or perish. For example, as their waterways have been rerouted, reticulated pythons have moved into cities such as Singapore and Bangkok. Other animals were introduced to cities on purpose or by accident. Honeybees were brought by settlers to many parts of the world. Butterflies brought themselves—**migrating** great distances to reach their roosts.

Urban life isn't always easy. There are dangers such as poisons, diseases, and pollution. There is the threat of death by predators, airplanes, vehicles, and other forces. There is competition for dinner and turf.

Yet, given the smallest chance—a park, a garden, a window box; a basement, a subway tunnel, a bridge—wildlife manages to survive in the city. Look around, and you may discover a host of animal neighbors you didn't even know were living next door.

Why should *they* be
       the only canines in the city—
those dogs so soft, so spoiled?
We have the stomach,
       we have the savvy
              to survive.
They were brought in style
       on cars or trains.
We came on foot,
       crossing dangerous terrains,
traveling decade after decade,
       mile after mile
from barren badlands
       through frozen forests
to these strange, crowded, concrete plains.
So, come on, give us welcome
       to rid you of your mice and rats.
Can't you forgive our taking
       those few occasional cats?

COYOTES
Chicago, Illinois

If you watch an old Western movie, you're likely to see and hear coyotes howling on the Great Plains. But these wild dogs are highly adaptable. They can live nearly anywhere and they eat almost anything. They now thrive all over North America, including major cities such as Chicago where, several years ago, sixty coyotes were fitted with radio collars to track their movements. They've even been known to hop on trains. In 2002, a coyote boarded a light-rail train in Portland, Oregon and snuggled up on the seats. It was removed by animal control before the train took off. In general, coyotes tend to avoid people. They usually prefer to hunt alone, most often at night, but they do form packs to defend territory. Their prey includes rodents and other small animals and sometimes household pets. That's why humane societies say it's best to keep dogs and cats indoors, safe from these skilled hunters.

7

Calm rivers, still lakes.
Nine months of warm. Night draws near.
Mosquitoes soon swarm.

Over the wide bridge,
people passing. Underneath,
spry bats, amassing.

MOSQUITOES AND MEXICAN FREE-TAILED BATS
Austin, Texas

There are about 3,500 species of mosquito in the world. The ones that people know best are the pests that feed on our blood. Some of those species are also infamous for carrying serious diseases such as malaria and yellow fever. Only the females bite, using their needle-like **proboscises** to pierce skin and suck up blood, their main diet. They need that blood to produce eggs.

Bats eat mosquitoes and other insects. Although these nocturnal mammals are found in many cities, the world's largest urban bat colony is found under the Ann W. Richards Congress Avenue Bridge in Austin, Texas. In March, the Mexican free-tailed bats migrate there from Mexico. During the summer months, between 750,000 to 1.5 million female bats and their offspring live beneath the bridge, emerging at dusk to feed on as much as 30,000 pounds of insects each night. Tourists and residents alike gather to watch the nightly show—and thank the bats for getting rid of those pesky mosquitoes.

For storks it doesn't pay to be aloof.
They choose a chimney, spire, roof
in the middle of town to raise their chicks
atop a messy nest of sticks.

For storks it doesn't come as any shock
to settle near a human flock.
Precarious perches seem alarming,
yet people also find them charming.

For years folks spread stories, sweet and weird,
until these birds became revered
as bringers of luck and sometimes maybe
the welcome gift of a newborn baby.

WHITE STORKS
Munster, France

The white stork is a legendary bird, thought to bring good luck—and also babies. Some stories say the birds found the infants in caves, carried them to houses, and dropped them down the chimneys. This myth possibly started because white storks have long nested on man-made structures such as chimneys, roofs, towers, steeples, and, more recently, power poles. White storks are long-distance migrants. In the spring, they fly to Europe to breed. In the late summer, they head to Africa to spend the winter. Sadly, their numbers have declined because of hunting, drought, collision with power lines, loss of wetlands, pollution, and use of pesticides. The town of Munster, in the Alsace-Lorraine region of France, created a successful repopulation program, to help the birds. They trained young storks not to migrate, and protected their nests. Recently, a similar program was started in Sussex, England, where storks have not bred in hundreds of years. If the program succeeds, perhaps the birds will once again nest in Storrington—"the village of storks"—which still features a pair of white storks on its emblem.

11

Marsupials can be problematic:
for example, take the brushtail possums.
They thump on your roof, enter your attic.
They eat your favorite fruits and blossoms.
They daily mark their turf with pungent scent.
At mating time they shriek to find a spouse.
They can become tenants who won't pay rent.
You don't want them to move into your house.
But you could offer shelter—it's not hard—
with just a box high on a sturdy tree
and you can fence off plants inside your yard
so herbivores will have to let them be.
You'll find it's worth a bit of time and labor
to make a possum a pleasant neighbor.

BRUSHTAIL POSSUMS
Sydney, Australia

Brushtail possums are **marsupials** that have adapted well to urban living. Strictly **herbivores**, they prefer to live in gardens and wooded areas where they can find leaves, flowers, and fruit to eat, or in houses near these areas. Once a possum (and its family) takes up residence in a house or yard, other possums will not move in. But possums in the attic can create problems. They are noisy, especially during the mating season, and they mark their territory with strong-smelling chemicals from glands in their chests and rear ends. Possums in the yard may annoy gardeners by eating their treasured plants. You need a special license to remove this protected animal from inside your home, and the animal must then be released on the same property because it will not survive elsewhere. Therefore, many people find it easier to fence off their plants and to set up an outdoor shelter for the possum. Good fences really can make good neighbors!

To pythons,
    water is water.
Rain drizzling gently,
    torrent pouring down.
A flooded rice paddy,
    a concrete storm drain.
A rush of run-off,
    a stand of muddy brown.
To pythons,
    water is water.
Stopping hearts and traffic,
    they take to country—and to town.
Monarchs of all urban snakes,
    pythons take the crown.

RETICULATED PYTHONS
Singapore

Singapore's widespread sewer system prevents tropical storms from flooding the city. It also allows reticulated pythons to travel through the city from neighboring forests and fields and to feed on rats, cats, and birds. In fact, the drain-and-canal system has replaced many of the rivers by which the pythons used to travel in search of food. These huge nonvenomous snakes, which can grow to over thirty feet in length, have adapted well to urban life. They can swim and climb, and they have heat-sensing pits near their mouths to find prey which they ambush and kill by constriction—they coil around their prey and squeeze, cutting off the blood supply to the victim's heart and brain. The Singapore Zoo receives hundreds of reticulated pythons every year from the public, wildlife rescue organizations, and pest removal services. Healthy snakes are generally released in nature reserves, where citizens hope they'll remain.

They like it warm. They like it dry.
They like it made of wood.
They don't need sun. They don't need sky.

A tree, a box, a shed—all good.
They also think a car is fine
Beneath the bonnet (that's the hood).

Under rocks, or down a mine,
These spiders do not grouse,
So long as they've the chance to dine

On beetle, cricket, gecko, mouse.
But if they're near and spring is here
They may crawl in your house.

These weathercasters have a reason:
They really hate the rainy season.

HUNTSMAN SPIDERS
Cape Town, South Africa

Most people have met spiders in their houses. These eight-legged **arthropods** move in because their insect prey has entered as well. Some spiders spin webs, while other species are ambush hunters, stalking their victims on the ground. Although the majority of spiders are venomous, most have venom that is too weak to affect humans or fangs too small to pierce skin. Only a few, such as the black widow, the Sydney funnel web, and the brown recluse, are dangerous to people. The huntsman spider is large and scary-looking but it's not deadly. In Cape Town and other parts of southern Africa, it is known as the "rain spider." It announces the start of the rainy season by taking shelter in buildings, cars, and other dry locations. Like its human hosts, this spider doesn't want to be caught in a downpour.

Give us
give us
what we want, what we need
bananas
peanuts
bread
or we'll take it
break it
shred your furniture, your papers
We'll claim your bed
Give us a temple
an office
a subway
a place to lay our head
You took our fruit trees
our forests
It's our turn to win
Give us
give us
Give up
Give in

18

RHESUS MONKEYS
New Delhi, India

Throughout India, monkeys have long been thought of as sacred animals. They are living representatives of the Hindu monkey god, Hanuman, who stands for strength and devotion. Rhesus monkeys live in temples throughout the country, where they are cared for and fed. Because of natural habitat loss, the release of monkeys by science labs, and other factors, there are now around 30,000 of these primates in New Delhi. They have created serious problems, such as breaking into and destroying homes and offices and harassing people to steal food. A deputy mayor of the city died from a fall off his balcony after a monkey attack. It is illegal to kill them, so officials have tried different ways to chase away the monkeys. But they haven't had much success. In the city of Jaipur, a group of monkeys took over a house and the people had to move out. The monkeys are now homeowners! But who can really blame them— they have nowhere else to go.

We want fish, we want meat.
Give us places to stay wet,
In the park—not the street.

You may watch while we eat
All the quarry we can get.
We want fish, we want meat.

We are lizards. We're not sweet.
Still and all, we're not a threat.
In the park—not the street—

We appreciate a treat.
Eggs are nice, but better yet,
We want fish, we want meat.

We can swim (but we can't sweat)
In the park—not the street.

Take a photo, send a tweet.
Don't attempt a friendly pet.
We want fish, we want meat
In the park—not the street.

WATER MONITORS
Bangkok, Thailand

Turtles and smaller reptiles often live in city parks. Bangkok's Lumpini Park is the home of a much larger reptile: a **carnivorous** alligator-sized lizard called the water monitor. These lizards have grown quite used to people. Visitors often bring bags of meat and fish to feed them. Good **scavengers**, the semi-aquatic water monitors live in other areas of the city as well. While the adults tend to be found in the water or on the grass, young monitors hide in the bushes and, if threatened, will climb into the trees. Protected by law,

these "dragons of Thailand" have few natural enemies, but they do fall prey to cars when they attempt to cross roads. In 2016, city officials moved many of the lizards to a wildlife sanctuary. The monitors had damaged some of the park's trees and plants. They also startled bicyclists, leading to accidents. However, thanks to their popularity with tourists, some monitors have been allowed to remain. And Thai citizens also appreciate their ability to rid the park of another urban animal—the rat.

21

It is possible they were there
    thousands of years ago
when the Romans first arrived.
It is possible they saw
    the Great Sewer being built
and somehow managed to stay
    and stay and stay in the Eternal City
while others of their kind
    vanished.
How they got there, who can say?
But here they are today,
    descendants of descendants
        of crabs that left the sea forever,
long-lived and robust,
beneath the beautiful ruins,
sitting under ancient stones,
scuttling through the dust.

RIVER CRABS
Rome, Italy

We usually think of crabs as sea creatures, but some crabs live in freshwater. Most of these can be found in wooded rivers, lakes, and streams. However, one amazing community thrives under the ruins of Emperor Trajan's Forum right in the center of Rome. No one is sure whether their ancestors were present before the Romans arrived thousands of years ago. It is possible that the crabs escaped from the nearby ancient fish market to breed in the underground canals connecting to one of the world's first sewer systems. Like other freshwater crabs, these Roman crabs feed mostly on insects, snails, and algae. But they are much larger than other crabs of the same species that live elsewhere. They grow more slowly and may live as many as five years longer. This may be because of their diet, the good quality of the water, and the lack of predators. Are these crabs a different species after all? Perhaps in time we'll find out.

It's a popular creature, the Brazilian agouti,
at home in a forest or a big city park.
Though not quite exactly what you'd call a beauty,
it's a popular creature, the Brazilian agouti,
Burying nuts (when it has too much booty),
that grow into trees is this rodent's trademark.
It's a popular creature, the Brazilian agouti,
at home in a forest or a big city park.

BRAZILIAN AGOUTIS
Rio de Janeiro, Brazil

Campo de Santana, a big park in the center of Rio de Janeiro, is home to ducks, swans, peacocks, and around one thousand Brazilian agoutis. These social rodents live in a wide variety of habitats from gardens to fields to rainforests. In the park, they are well-supplied with nuts and fruits. But in the wild, they have to gather their own, and in doing so, they perform a unique service—growing Brazil nut trees. With their strong teeth, agoutis are one of the only animals able to bite through the thick pods that hold the nuts, which they then bury. Like squirrels, the agoutis will dig up some of the nuts to eat, but others will be left to sprout. Recently, scientists gathered several of the Campo de Santana agoutis and released them into Tijuca National Park, where agoutis once lived. This huge rainforest, located in the heart of Rio, has grown back over abandoned sugarcane and coffee plantations. Scientists hope the agoutis will repopulate the forest and help to raise many new and valuable Brazil nut trees.

Country
bees like meadows,
but here in town a pot
or two of fragrant lavender
will do.

HONEYBEES
Vancouver, Canada

The honeybee was introduced to North America in the 1600s by European settlers who practiced apiculture (beekeeping) to produce honey. The bees thrived all over the continent, wherever there was nectar to be found. Recently, the insects have been suffering from colony collapse disorder—the sudden disappearance of worker bees from a hive. No one is sure why this is happening. Scientists have suggested several possible causes, including mites, fungus, the use of pesticides, and the commercial beekeeping practice of frequently moving the hives, which exposes them to stress and disease. This is a serious problem for humans as well because many of the world's crops are **pollinated** by these insects. Urban bees, however, seem to do better, possibly because urban apiculture uses better practices. Until a few years ago, many cities, such as Vancouver, banned beekeeping. Now there are bees on the roof of Vancouver City Hall.

After such a long and perilous journey
across wild mountains, tame gardens, familiar parks, and distant plains,
they leave behind
the trail of sweet-nectared flowers,
grateful for
their needed winter's rest in Butterfly Town,
hanging from the eucalyptus, still as dead leaves.
We tourists pause to marvel at these precious pollinators
at last taking time off from work.

At last taking time off from work,
we tourists pause to marvel at these precious pollinators,
hanging from the eucalyptus, still as dead leaves
(their needed winter's rest in Butterfly Town),
grateful for
the trail of sweet-nectared flowers
they leave behind
across wild mountains, tame gardens, familiar parks, and distant plains
after such a long and perilous journey.

MONARCH BUTTERFLIES
Pacific Grove, California

Monarchs are known for long migrations across many **terrains**, including cities and towns. No single butterfly makes the entire trip. As the weather gets warmer, the monarchs move north, laying eggs on the way. They can create up to four new generations of butterflies. Each generation makes part of the northern journey, facing challenges such as bad weather, fatigue, food shortages, airplanes, and cars. The butterflies pause to feed on nectar from a variety of flowers. They pollinate some of these blossoms, helping the plants reproduce. When summer ends, the last generation of monarchs born head south for the winter, gathering in sites such as George Washington Park in the town of Pacific Grove, California. Tourists visit this sanctuary to see the butterflies resting in the eucalyptus trees. This generation may live a total of seven months or more. In the spring, it will begin the northward migration, producing more beautiful butterflies and a trail of lovely flowers.

Thanks for knocking down that wall.
Thanks for your delicious corn.
We declare a free-for-all.

Thanks for graveyard, shopping mall.
Thanks for football field we've torn.
Thanks for knocking down that wall.

Thanks for every fast food stall,
Each playground where these shoats were born.
We declare a free-for-all.

We don't really like to brawl
(though if forced, we will—we warn).
Thanks for knocking down that wall.

Thanks for acorns in the fall.
Thanks for grubs we ate this morn.
We declare a free-for-all.

Enjoy us for our utter gall
(and our bristles that you've shorn).
Thanks for knocking down that wall.
We declare a free-for-all.

WILD BOARS
Berlin, Germany

In 1961, a wall was built to divide Germany's East and West Berlin. The east was under the control of the former Soviet Union; the west was allied with the U.S., Britain, and France. In 1989, the Wall was torn down. Citizens could now travel freely between East and West Berlin. Other creatures enjoyed this freedom too. Wild boars from neighboring forests were drawn to the city, particularly for its food. They now number in the thousands. The boars have created problems ranging from traffic accidents to destruction of cemeteries, football fields, and shops. Though they are smart and generally peaceful, they will sometimes attack. The males use their tusks as weapons if they are cornered, and the females have been known to slam into anything that threatens their piglets or shoats (older piglets). Authorities have tried to limit their numbers through licensed hunting and other methods, yet the population is increasing, and some citizens want stricter controls. But the animals have their supporters as well. One gentleman had a boar climb into his car and lay its head in his lap. He's a fan for life.

31

Unwelcome:
These skeleton-makers.
Uninvited:
These bone-breakers.
Except here
   in this ancient walled city
where the hyena men feed
   these not-dogs, not-cats,
   sometimes calling them by name
   (though they're never really tame).
Where they say, "Here's meat.
   Don't eat my lamb, my calf."
And these not-dogs, not-cats
   mostly agree.
They do not utter thank you.
They surely never laugh.

HYENAS
Harar, Ethiopia

The spotted hyena is not welcome in most African cities. Though it is famed as a scavenger, it is more often a fearsome hunter. Its "laugh" is a call of excitement or nervousness, often used to tell members of its pack, "Go away! Leave me alone with my food!" Packs of spotted hyenas can take down a zebra, a wildebeest, or another large animal with ease. As farms and towns invaded their territory, these predators began to hunt livestock, pets, and even humans. But in Ethiopia, one place welcomes hyenas—the ancient walled city of Harar. Centuries ago, leaders of the city decided that if they left out scraps of meat for the hyenas, they would not attack people or livestock. The plan worked. Today, a small group of "hyena men" feed the animals, sometimes as a show for tourists. They may offer the meat by hand or even mouth-to-mouth on a stick. The hyena men respect these animals and work to earn their trust. They know that these large and fierce creatures will never ever be pets.

We sing in the gutter, we sing in the drain
How our voices amplify!
City canyons filled with rain.
We sing in the gutter, we sing in the drain.
We do not sing to entertain.
We're seeking mates, and that is why
We sing in the gutter, we sing in the drain.
How our voices amplify!

MIEN-TIEN TREE FROGS
Taipei, Taiwan

When a male frog calls to attract a mate, loud and long is usually good. Louder and longer might be better, which is what Mien-tien tree frogs seem to be trying in Taipei. Most frogs have balloon-like vocal sacs to increase the volume of their sounds. Mien-tien tree frogs amplify their calls even further—they sing from the open concrete storm drains, common throughout the city.

But there are dangers in the drains. When a female frog picks a male, he hops onto her back, and the drain's slippery walls make it hard for the pair to scramble out. Predators such as frog-eating snakes often lurk in these "urban canyons." So the male frogs perch on branches and other objects to keep watch, and also to help them exit. Scientists hope they will eventually discover if these frogs are more successful at attracting mates than their relatives that do their courting on patches of dry land.

Burrowing beneath graves,
  they topple headstones,
    unearth bones that have not stirred
      in one hundred years.

Unwitting vandals,
  they mean no harm.

A city cemetery is a fine place
      to be alive
  if you are a badger.

Though their descendants may rightly be disturbed,
    the long departed are likely not perturbed.

BADGERS
Swindon, England

The Eurasian badger is a beloved creature in stories, films, and often in real life—except when it wrecks cemeteries, overturning gravestones and digging up bones. Swindon, among other U.K. towns, is suffering from this mammal's unfortunate habit. Badgers live in complex burrows called "setts." These setts have many entrances, tunnels, and chambers. Besides digging the burrows, badgers also dig for worms, roots, bulbs, and other food. It's their need to dig that causes accidental damage to cemeteries. Badgers are a protected species and cannot be removed from their territory, so churches and town councils are trying to find ways to stop this damage. Ideas include fencing and one-way doors that allow badgers to exit but not reenter their setts. Church officials have also created "bone patrols" to gather and rebury unearthed bones in new graves. But the badgers continue to dig. One burrowed into the stonework of a 500-year-old Scottish castle. The lone animal proved much more destructive than many of the castle's previous guests!

It's said that long ago a god appeared
atop a mountain, riding a white deer.
Today each doe, fawn, and buck is revered.
They roam the storied streets. They're welcome here.

From all over the world, visitors throng.
to see the town, its park and sacred shrine,
to feed these creatures, twelve hundred strong,
that aren't patient, that will not wait in line.

At vending machines and food carts, they flock.
Some bow for biscuits—a delightful trick—
while others are testy, inclined to shock.
They jostle. They nip. They head-butt. They kick.

But greet them kindly and do not tease them.
Keep calm, bow first, and that may well please them.

SIKA DEER
Nara, Japan

Nara is a Japanese city known for its shrines and temples, its park, and its more than one thousand deer. There is a legend that a god appeared on a white deer to protect the town. Since then Sika deer have been regarded as sacred animals. To show respect for these creatures, people often bow to them. Many of the deer have learned to bow back—usually for food. Visitors can purchase special crackers to feed the animals, adding to their diet of leaves, fruit, nuts, and seeds. Although most are calm, some of the deer can get quite demanding. They will pull people's clothes, chew on cameras, bite, kick, or head-butt to get those crackers. Others have wandered off and caused damage to farmers' crops. The Japanese government has issued tips on how to deal with the deer and has also rounded up deer that have strayed too far from town. It wants to ensure that both the citizens and the thirteen thousand annual visitors can take delight in the country's national treasure.

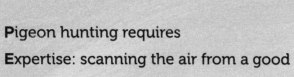

Pigeon hunting requires
Expertise: scanning the air from a good
Roost—perhaps atop the
Empire State Building,
George Washington Bridge, or
Riverside Church.
Imitations of cliffs, ledges, mountains—
Natural perches the birds once favored long before these towering
Edifices arose.

Fierce flying, too, is needed for the chase.
Aerial acrobatics
Leading up to furious acceleration, that death-defying dive,
Clocking in at 200 miles per hour.
On target. On point.
Nearer, nearer, and...

Strike!

PIER 17

PEREGRINE FALCONS
New York, New York

The peregrine falcon is not only one of the world's fastest birds—when it dives to catch prey, it's the fastest animal on Earth. It can reach a speed of 200 miles per hour! In the middle of the 20th century, this magnificent bird disappeared from much of its range because of a pesticide known as DDT. This chemical weakened the birds' eggshells so that they cracked when the parents sat on the eggs. After DDT was largely banned in the 1970s, the birds were reintroduced to the East Coast of the U.S. Peregrine falcons traditionally nest on cliffs and in the mountains. But many of the reintroduced birds and their offspring moved into cities such as New York, choosing to nest on skyscraper ledges and bridge supports. They can even be found on the Empire State Building! Besides having good nesting sites, cities have other advantages, too. They have high and wide flyways, lots of light by which to see prey, and a supply of one of the peregrine's favorite foods—pigeons. Today, the peregrine population seems to be increasing. City living suits this falcon very well indeed.

When you
travel to a
distant city and miss
your own, look for pigeons to take
you home.

Pecking,
cooing, bowing,
wooing, they make the strange
familiar wherever you
may roam.

PIGEONS
Everywhere

Pigeons are ancient and adaptable birds. Thousands of years ago, people domesticated them for food and feathers. Because pigeons can find their way home over hundreds of miles, they have long been used to carry messages. When the first Olympic Games were held, pigeons carried news of the winners. During the first and second World Wars, the birds were heroes, transporting messages across enemy lines. European settlers brought pigeons with them to America. Escaped birds bred and thrived in cities here, as they did on other continents. Today, they live and nest on buildings, bridges, and other structures just as their ancestors did on high cliffs and rocky ledges. Some people welcome the sight of these birds; others call them "flying rats." Whether you love them or hate them, rock pigeons are now and forever a familiar sight all over the world.

43

Poetry forms

Some of the poems in this book, such as "Coyotes," "Rhesus Monkeys," "River Crabs," "Hyenas," and "Badgers," are written in free (non-rhyming) verse or a combination of free verse and rhyme, often with a couplet (two rhyming lines) at the end. Others, including "Where Life's No Longer Wild" and "White Storks" are in rhymed couplets. Still others feature forms with stricter rules. Take a look at the different types on this page.

Triolet

Brazilian Agoutis;
Mien-tien Tree Frogs

An eight-line poem with just two rhymes: ABaAabAB. The first, fourth, and seventh lines repeat and so do the second and eighth.

Haiku

Mosquitoes and Mexican
Free-Tailed Bats

A traditional form in Japan, the haiku focuses on capturing a moment, often in nature. English versions of the haiku have three lines, with five syllables in the first, seven in the second, and five in the third.

Cinquain

Honeybees; Pigeons

A five-line poem with two syllables in line one, four in line two, six in line three, eight in line four, and two in line five.

Reverso

Monarch Butterflies

A poem with two halves. The second half reverses the lines of the first half, with changes only in punctuation and capitalization, and says something different from the first half.

Villanelle
Water Monitors; Wild Boars

A nineteen-line French form of five tercets (three-line linked verses) and a quatrain (four lines with a set rhyme scheme). It has two refrains—repeated lines—and two rhymes. The complex scheme is:

Refrain 1 (A1)
Line 2 (b)
Refrain 2 (A2)
Line 4 (a)
Line 5 (b)
Refrain 1 (A1)
Line 7 (a)
Line 8 (b)
Refrain 2 (A2)
Line 10 (a)
Line 11 (b)
Refrain 1 (A1)
Line 13 (a)
Line 14 (b)
Refrain 2 (A2)
Line 16 (a)
Line 17 (b)
Refrain 1 (A1)
Refrain 2 (A2)

Acrostic
Peregrine Falcons

In this form, the first, last, or another letter runs down the poem to spell out a word or words, perhaps the title.

Sonnet
Brushtail Possums; Sika Deer

A fourteen-line poem made up of four quatrains and a couplet. To show a rhyme scheme, give each new rhyme a letter. The first time the rhyme is introduced, it gets a capital letter. So "A" rhymes with "a," "B" with "b," etc. The Shakespearean sonnet's rhyme scheme is ABab CDcd EFef Gg. Each line is written in iambic pentameter—ten syllables, with the accent on the second, fourth, sixth, eighth, and tenth syllables.

Terza rima
Huntsman Spiders

An Italian form made of tercets and, sometimes, a final couplet. There is no limit to the number of verses, but their rhyme scheme is fixed: ABa, bCb, cDc, dEd, etc.

Author's note

I've been a bird watcher for a long time. Some people are still surprised when I tell them about all of the species I've seen in Brooklyn, New York, where I've lived for many years. So it's funny that I was surprised to discover the many other animals that live in my city and in cities all over the world.

When I realized that creatures once known for living only in the wild were now urban dwellers, I began to investigate. I read about them, looked at photos and films, and talked to zoologists from around the globe. I traveled, too, visiting parks and other places to see some of these creatures firsthand —the bats in Austin; the butterflies in Pacific Grove. One day, I watched a peregrine falcon eating a pigeon on the roof of the Brooklyn Museum! As a result of this research, I knew I wanted to write a book about them. At first
I thought it would be only in prose. But soon I began to hear the voices of those critters, began to see lyrical images of them—wily monkeys in New Delhi, surprising crabs in Rome, fearless Sika deer in Japan—and a collection of poems began to take shape. These poems featured a variety of species, some familiar, some not, in places both famous and little known.

I hope to see more of these animals someday—and that perhaps my readers will as well. Most of all, I hope that we will all appreciate the life around us and do our best to protect our animal neighbors in cities— and in the wild.

Marilyn Singer

Glossary

adaptation the process that allows animals to fit better into an environment; it may include changes to a species' body or behavior or both.

arthropod an animal with jointed legs and a hard outer covering called an exoskeleton, but no backbone.

carnivore a meat-eating animal; the adjective is carnivorous.

herbivore a plant-eating animal; the adjective is herbivorous.

marsupial a type of mammal that carries and feeds its young in its pouch.

migration the movement of animals from one place to another, often during spring or fall, to find food, escape difficult weather, and/or to breed.

pollination the transfer of pollen by bees, other insects, birds, and some mammals from the male parts of a flower to the female parts in order to produce more plants.

proboscis the tube-like mouthparts of some insects, used for sucking up nectar, blood, or other food; in some species it is needle-like to pierce skin.

scavenger an animal that feeds on dead or decaying material, or on food thrown away by humans.

terrain land or ground, or its geographical features, as in "rocky terrain."

Find out more

Books

Downer, Ann, *Wild Animal Neighbors: Sharing Our Urban World*. Minneapolis, MN: Twenty-First Century Books, 2014.

Feinstein, Julie, *Field Guide to Urban Wildlife*. Mechanicsburg, PA: Stackpole Books, 2011.

Hodgkins, Fran, *Animals Among Us*. North Haven, CT: Linnet Books, 2000.

Websites

www.celebrateurbanbirds.org

www.getaway.co.za/wildlife/animals-living-in-cities

www.theguardian.com/environment/2017/may/20/urban-beasts-how-wild-animals-have-moved-into-cities

www.theguardian.com/environment/2015/mar/08/urban-wildlife-animals-in-city

news.nationalgeographic.com/2016/04/160418-animals-urban-cities-wildlife-science-coyotes

news.nationalgeographic.com/2018/05/urban-living-drives-evolution-in-surprising-way

www.nytimes.com/2017/05/02/travel/safari-city-guide-urban-wildlife-ecosystems-viewing.html

TV shows

Cities: Nature's New Wild, BBC, 2018

Planet Earth II, Episode 6: Cities, BBC, 2016

Organizations

Bat Conservation International: www.batcon.org

City Wild Life, Washington, D.C.: www.citywildlife.org

Urban Bird Foundation: www.urbanbird.org

Urban Rivers: www.urbanriv.org

Urban Wildlife Conservation Program: www.fws.gov/urban

The Urban Wildlife Working Group: www.urbanwildlifegroup.org

Xerces Society for Invertebrate Conservation: www.xerces.org

All web adresses were correct at the time of printing.
The Publishers and Author cannot be held responsible
for the content of the websites referred to in this book.

48